Magic...Naturally!

VICKI COBB

Magic...Naturally!

Science Entertainments & Amusements

REVISED EDITION

illustrated by Lionel Kalish

■ HarperCollins*Publishers*

Library of Congress Cataloging-in-Publication Data
Cobb, Vicki.
    Magic . . . naturally! : science entertainments & amusements / by
Vicki Cobb with illustrations by Lionel Kalish. — Rev. ed.
        p.   cm.
    Includes index.
    Summary: Explains and demonstrates scientific principles by
using them to create magic tricks.
    ISBN 0-06-022474-6. — ISBN 0-06-022475-4 (lib. bdg.)
    1. Science—Experiments—Juvenile literature.
2. Conjuring—Juvenile literature.   [1. Magic tricks.]
I. Kalish, Lionel, ill. II. Title.
Q164.C49   1993   90-21829
793.8—dc20   CIP
                                                            AC

CONTENTS

Magic...Naturally!

BE PHENOMENAL!

Want to amaze and mystify your friends? Want to amuse and entertain them by doing the impossible? Be a magician. Appear to defy natural laws by performing incredible feats. Seem to bend nature to your will. Best of all, have fun learning your tricks by learning some secrets of nature.

Nature is a fabulous magician. Imagine putting a solid white object into a transparent liquid and watching it disappear before your very eyes. Amazing! Or is it? Actually, you do it every time you put a lump of sugar into a cup of tea. You can make clever use of a lump of sugar and its natural behavior in your magic act.

Suppose you use the lump of sugar to hold a

spring in a coiled position. You put the sugar and the spring into a teacup (without letting anyone see what you're doing) and rest a spoon on the sugar cube. Then, when you pour on hot water and let nature do its thing, you create magic. The sugar dissolves, releasing the spring. Your audience sees you pour hot water into a cup and, suddenly, the spoon jumps out. Magic . . . naturally!

This book contains instructions for performing some amusing, puzzling, and exciting magic tricks. All of them are based on science. Some were known by conjurers hundreds of years ago. Others come from more recent scientific discoveries. You can learn the amazing science behind them all.

You can have fun by yourself learning the tricks in this book. But the only thing that will make you a performer is practice. Also, there are no rules to tell you just how to be entertaining. The best advice is to practice a trick until you feel comfortable with it. You might want to try it a few times in front of a mirror. Choose the time and place for the performance of a trick carefully. Sometimes you might want to perform on the spur of the moment. Other times you might want to put together several tricks for a magic show.

4

Make up stories or tell jokes as you do your tricks. Bring your own personality to your act. I've included a few performance tips, but the most important thing is to bring yourself to your act. After you go public, you'll learn from your audience the things that work as entertainment.

A few words of warning. Some of the tricks involve using the stove or a flame. Some involve substances that are poisonous or that may be highly flammable or harmful to your skin or eyes or clothes. Wash your hands carefully after using them. **Check with an adult before beginning any experiment.** Read all labels carefully and follow the directions in this book step by step. Don't mix household chemicals unless you understand the dangers and have an adult present. If you follow these rules, you will not be in danger. As a reminder, these symbols will appear in the Setup sections of the tricks:

◆   FLAME

☠   POISON

�   FUMES

▲   DAMAGE TO SKIN, EYES, OR CLOTHES

One last thing. Once you know how to do a trick, the mystery will be gone for you. You may be surprised to see how easy it is to make others wonder. Keeping an audience guessing is one of the chief ingredients of magic, and professional magicians have sworn not to tell their audiences what makes their tricks work. However, you might want to make an exception to this rule when performing the tricks in this book. One of the exciting things about these tricks is understanding the science behind them. You can make your performance even more entertaining by asking your friends if they can figure out why a trick works and then letting them in on the explanation after you've kept them guessing for a while.

This book will start you on an adventure. It's an opening to science, entertainment, and magic— a natural combination if there ever was one. Make it happen.

MECHANICAL WIZARDRY

A ball is thrown into the air and never returns to earth. Would you believe your eyes? Or would you think, "This doesn't make sense. There's a trick here someplace"? Magicians and scientists both know that we can be fooled.

Galileo, a scientist who lived in Italy in the sixteenth to seventeenth centuries, questioned what he saw when he looked at a rolling ball. He saw that a ball rolling along the ground finally comes to a stop. He said to himself, "This doesn't make sense. A rolling ball should not stop rolling."

Here's his reasoning: A ball that rolls down a hill picks up speed, going faster and faster. A ball rolling uphill rolls more and more slowly until it stops for an instant before rolling back down the hill. A ball rolling on level ground should not speed up (because it's not rolling downhill), and it should not slow down (because it's not rolling uphill). A ball rolling on level ground should keep rolling at the same speed forever. Since it does stop rolling, Galileo figured there must be something else happening. Something must be slowing the ball down.

Physics is the science that grew from the kinds of questions Galileo asked. The part of physics that deals with the motion of balls and other inanimate objects is called *mechanics.* The natural laws of mechanics describe how objects move and how forces upon them change the ways they move. More than once they show that you can't always believe what you see. Now you can use them to create unbelievable illusions.

★

PULLING OFF THE IMPOSSIBLE: INERTIA AND FRICTION

Challenge a friend to remove a strip of paper that is between a stack of checkers and the cap of a catsup bottle. The checkers may not be touched or caused to topple. Result: crash after crash. Then you, a true believer in natural law, pull off the job.

The Setup and the Act

☆ a strip of paper about 1 ½ inches wide and 3 inches long
☆ a catsup bottle with a cap
☆ stackable objects such as checkers, poker chips, or quarters

Place the strip of paper on top of the capped bottle so that one end is longer than the other. Stack objects on top of the paper, making a big show of how easy it is to knock them over. As long as there is some stability to the stack, a higher stack works better and makes the trick look more difficult. Challenge someone in your audience to remove the strip without knocking over the objects. After each attempt fails, set the stack up again.

To remove the strip, moisten your index finger (so it briefly sticks to the paper, providing better contact), grasp the longer end of the paper between your index finger and thumb, and bring your hand down, toward the tabletop, quickly. The trick is to move the strip out from under the checkers as fast as possible. So if you hesitate, you too will fail.

Performance Tips: This is a good trick to perform for a friend in an informal manner. You can also use it effectively in a tabletop show for a small audience.

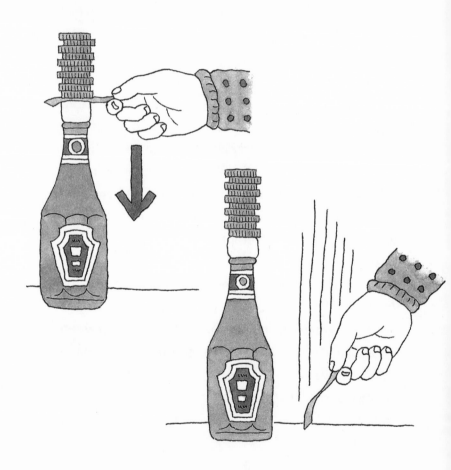

What's Really Happening

Galileo not only wondered why rolling balls stopped rolling. He also wondered why resting objects remained at rest. Years later, an Englishman named Isaac Newton came up with an answer to both questions. His theory is called *Newton's First Law of Motion.* It states: Moving objects will remain in the state of motion and resting objects will remain at rest unless an outside force acts upon them.

The outside force that makes a ball rolling on a level surface stop rolling is *friction.* Friction is the force that makes two touching surfaces resist moving past each other. The friction between the bottom checker on the stack and the paper it rests on is strong enough to cause the checkers to fall when the paper moves.

Suppose you could eliminate the friction between the paper and the bottom checker. What would happen to the stack? The answer is: nothing. There is no force directly acting on the checkers, so they won't move. Get rid of the friction and the checkers stay in place.

It's easy enough to think away friction. In the real world it doesn't work quite that way. One way to reduce friction is to use a lubricant, such as oil, between two surfaces. Another way is to make both surfaces very smooth. In this trick you reduce friction by moving the paper very quickly. The less time the two surfaces are in contact, the less friction there is.

Variety Acts

Fill a glass two thirds full of water and cover it with a playing card. Balance an egg, with the larger end down, in a ring of aluminum foil on the card.

Place yc . middle finger against your thumb, then flick the card out from under the egg. The sharp blow makes the card fly off. The egg falls into the water unbroken. Break the egg later to prove it was not hard-boiled.

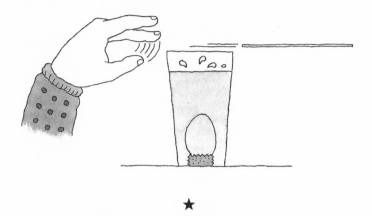

★

Make a ring of stiff paper by gluing the ends together. Make it the same size as the top of a catsup bottle. Put the ring on top of an opened catsup bottle, and rest the cap on top of the ring. With a flick of a pencil (or a wand) whisk the ring away. The cap drops neatly on top of the open bottle.

On a smooth surface, stack ten black checkers and one red checker, placing the red checker second from the bottom. Stand another red checker on its edge and shoot it at the stack by pressing on the top and then letting your finger slide down around the edge. The checker should scoot out from under your finger. With practice, you can make a direct hit so that the curved side of the moving checker delivers a blow to the red checker in the pile. The red checker is knocked from the pile without disturbing the black checkers.

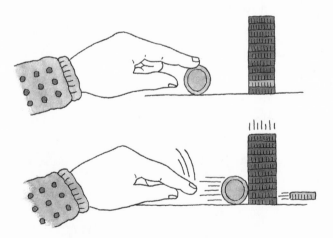

★
KARATE PAYOFF:
THE INSIDE STORY ON FORCE

A swift karate chop with a dollar bill breaks a pencil in two. But your friends quickly learn that money has that kind of power for you alone.

The Setup and the Act

☆   a long wooden pencil
☆   a dollar bill
☆   a willing friend

Announce you can break a pencil with a dollar bill. In an open manner, fold the bill in half lengthwise. Ask a friend to hold the pencil securely at either end. Make sure his or her grip is firm.

Hold the folded bill at one end between your thumb and the first joint of your index finger. Your hand should be a loosely curled fist.

To dramatize the feat, raise and lower the bill over the pencil twice while counting, "One . . . two . . ." As you bring your hand down on the count of three, straighten your index finger so you can deliver a karate chop to the pencil. Be sure to move your hand as swiftly as possible and don't hesitate before impact. Be sure to curl your index finger again after the blow has been delivered so your audience won't guess how you broke the pencil.

Invite others to try to duplicate your feat with another pencil.

Performance Tips: Practice karate chopping pencils without the bill until you are confident. Then practice with a bill so you can get the timing of extending and withdrawing your finger. This trick is good for spontaneous, casual fun with a friend as well as for an informal show.

What's Really Happening

A force has two parts to it. One part is the mass of the object delivering the force. The other part is the change in speed of the object after it delivers the force. It's easy to see how a large object like a sledgehammer can deliver a larger force than the household variety hammer. But a small object like a bullet can shatter a brick because it is traveling so fast.

A karate chop is a force delivered by the hand, which doesn't have a lot of mass, moving as fast as it can. People with training in karate can use the hand to deliver a blow so swiftly that the force on impact can be great enough to break a brick or a block of wood. When the struck object breaks, the hand is not injured since it doesn't receive the force of the blow. But if the struck object doesn't break, the hand does receive the painful force of the blow. So in this trick, you won't hurt your finger if you keep it moving swiftly.

★

SUPER-TOUGH TISSUE PAPER: A NONELASTIC COLLISION

Would you believe you can use all your strength to ram a tightly stretched piece of tissue paper with a broomstick and it <u>will not tear</u>? Your friends won't take your word for it. Read on.

The Setup and the Act

- ☆ tissue paper
- ☆ a cardboard tube from a roll of paper towels
- ☆ a rubber band
- ☆ salt
- ☆ the handle from a broom

Separate the two plies of the tissue in front of your audience. Be sure to display them so everyone sees how delicate they are. Stretch a single ply over one end of the cardboard tube and hold it in place with a rubber band. Pour in salt to a depth of at least four inches.

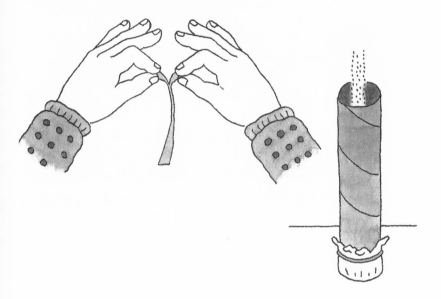

Announce that you will ram the broomstick down the tube without breaking the tissue. Then do so with all your strength. (Hamming it up a bit here can add to the show.) Invite others to try. No one will be strong enough.

21

Performance Tips: Some tissues are stronger than others. Practice this trick before you try it in front of friends. You may find you'll have to use both plies if the tissue is very delicate. But try adding more salt before you decide to use unseparated tissue.

What's Really Happening

When a cue ball in a billiard game collides in a direct hit with a resting ball, the collision transfers motion. After impact, the resting ball moves away, reaching almost the speed the cue ball had before the collision, and the cue ball is at rest. A collision where no motion is lost is called an *elastic collision.* As collisions go, in our imperfect world, an encounter between billiard balls is pretty elastic.

Not all collisions are elastic and transfer motion. Throw a wad of modeling clay on the floor. It doesn't bounce and nothing moves. Instead, the energy of motion is used to change the shape of the clay.

In this trick, the tissue paper is protected by salt crystals, a material that absorbs the total force of the collision. Here's how it works. There are a great many tiny air spaces between the salt crystals. On impact, the salt grains are packed closer together. This absorbs the force of the collision, so there's no force left to tear the paper.

★
THE HAUNTED HANKY:
LEVITATION WITH A LEVER

An ordinary bandanna takes on a life of its own as it falls and rises at your command.

The Setup and the Act

☆ a bandanna about 22 inches wide on each side, made of a material you can't see through

☆ a needle

☆ thread the same color as the bandanna

☆ paper drinking straws

Turn up one side of the bandanna ⅜ inch. Stitch along the edge, leaving both ends open. This kind of hem is called a casing. The casing should be

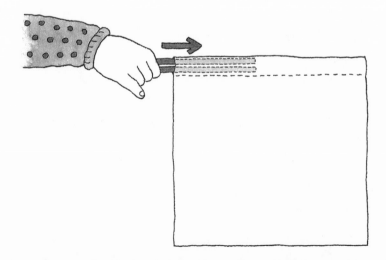

just wide enough to allow you to insert two flattened paper drinking straws side by side. Insert the straws in one side of the casing, pushing them in just far enough so they can't be seen. The straws will stiffen about half the length of the casing.

Before your act, fold the bandanna in a triangle with the straws forming part of the point. Tie the bandanna around your neck. The casing with the straws should lie flat on your back.

As a part of your act, untie the bandanna and hold it by the two corners of the casing with the straws to your right. (Reverse these directions if you're left-handed.) Without moving your hands

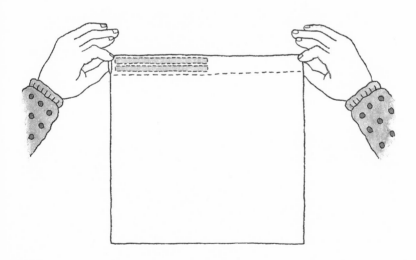

together, show your audience both sides of the bandanna. Drop the right-hand corner and let the bandanna fall, still holding the other corner with your left hand. Tie a large knot in the bandanna near the left-hand corner.

Hold the knotted part with your left hand and pull the handkerchief through your right hand with a gentle motion. Then hold the knotted part with

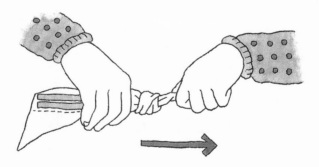

your right hand and make the same stroking motion once or twice with your left hand. At the end of

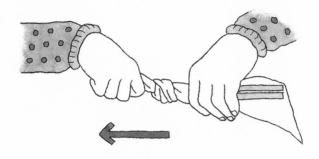

the final stroke, hold the bandanna with your left hand and let go with your right. The straws will hold it upright in the air. Now slide your left thumb

over your left index finger in a small motion that moves the bottom of the straws. The straws are stiff enough to slowly lower the handkerchief and raise it again. A little practice before you perform this for anyone will quickly show you the right moves. No one will notice the small motion you must make, because they will be watching the large motion made by the other end of the straws. If you wave your right hand in a magical way as you command the hanky to rise and fall, the illusion of levitation is complete.

When you have finished, untie the knot, roll the bandanna into a ball, and stuff it into a pocket. The paper straws are permanently crumpled, so this trick can't be repeated without preparing the setup again.

Performance Tips: There's nothing quite like the unexpected, seemingly casual event of a magic trick. Wear the bandanna to school one day. Then, at the right moment, perhaps at lunch, go into your act in an offhand way. Your friends will be used to seeing the bandanna around your neck and will have no idea that you have spent time preparing for this moment.

What's Really Happening

A rod-shaped object that turns around a point, called a *lever*, is a useful tool for moving objects. A seesaw is a lever with its turning point, called the *fulcrum*, in its center.

A crowbar is a lever with the fulcrum much closer to one end of the rod than the other. When you push down the longer end of the crowbar, the shorter end moves up a shorter distance. But the force that this short distance can apply is multiplied. It can be strong enough to pry nails from wood.

A lever with a fulcrum close to one end can also be used to make the long end move faster than the short end. Baseball bats and fishing rods are levers that magnify a small motion on the short end to produce a longer and faster motion on the other end. This is what the straws do in your trick. Your lever is hidden in the casing. But you can manipulate one end with a small, unnoticeable motion that produces a large, magical motion on the other end.

★

THE STRANGE STRAW: A SHIFT IN THE CENTER OF GRAVITY

You pass out drinking straws to your friends and ask them to balance the straw across a finger. Your friends discover that they must put a finger under the center of the straw. Then you do a balancing act with your finger obviously off-center. Curious, how strange it looks.

The Setup and the Act

☆ a box of paper or plastic straws
☆ a tiny lead fishing weight

Put the fishing weight in the end of one of the straws. It should fit snugly so it won't come loose.

Put the straw back in the box, making a mental note of its exact position. Close the box and, if it came with a cellophane wrapper, see if you can replace the wrapper to make it look as if the box is brand-new.

Open the box of straws and pass a few out to your friends. Ask them to balance the straws across their index fingers. Then you remove the straw with the weight and place it across your finger. (You should practice beforehand so you know exactly where to place your finger.) The straw will be perfectly balanced with your finger fairly close to the end with the weight. You can also rest the straw at the edge of a table with the unweighted end sticking way out in the air.

Performance Tips: This is a good trick to spring on friends when they come over to your house and you're having refreshments.

What's Really Happening

An empty seesaw is balanced when the fulcrum is in the center. That's because the seesaw has a regular shape and its weight is evenly distributed along its length. The place where you put a fulcrum so a lever is balanced is the lever's *center of gravity.*

If you put a weight on only one end of a seesaw, you can balance it again in one of two ways: (1) By putting an equal weight on the other end. (2) By moving the fulcrum to the new center of gravity, which is closer to the end with the weight. Some seesaws have notches in the center so the fulcrum can be adjusted for people of different weights at each end.

A straw, like a seesaw board, has a center of gravity at its center. But the lead weight secretly changes the center of gravity so you appear to be doing an impossible balancing act when you change the fulcrum.

FLUID
FASCINATIONS

For magicians, there's nothing quite like an invisible assistant, and nature has provided one. It's handy, creeping into every space not already occupied by something else, and it moves easily. Not only can't you see it, you can't smell or taste it either.

In case you haven't already guessed, air is this invisible natural wonder. Air is a gas, a kind of *matter*, which is the stuff of our universe. Matter exists in three forms: solid, liquid, and gas. A solid has a definite size and shape. But liquids and gases, called *fluids* (from a Latin word meaning "to flow"), take on the shapes of their containers. A liquid has a definite volume; it takes the shape of its container, except for its top surface. A gas does not have a definite volume. It takes on both the shape and volume of its container, spreading out to fill it completely.

Air and water are the fluids we know best. They have some surprising properties that will enhance your act. Discover their amazing ways.

★

HEAVY READING: THE WEIGHT OF AIR

The blow of a broomstick breaks a slat of wood sticking out from the edge of a table. No big deal. But wait . . . the wood is held in place with nothing more than two sheets of newspaper. Now news is not a weighty matter—or is it?

The Setup and the Act

☆ an inexpensive foot-long ruler or a thin slat of wood
☆ two sheets of a large-sized newspaper
☆ a broomstick

Place the slat of wood on a table with half of it sticking out over the edge. Show your audience

how the wood flips off the table if you strike it
without holding it down.

Reposition the slat and place two opened sheets
of newspaper over the part of the slat that is on
the table. Smooth out the paper with your hands
so as little air as possible remains between the
paper and the tabletop. (The smoother the tabletop, the better the seal under the newspaper. This
trick doesn't work as well on a tablecloth.)

Deliver a blow to the wood with the broomstick in a swift karate chop. The idea is to deliver the force so swiftly that the wood is broken before it has a chance to act as a lever and lift the paper. If air has time to get under the paper, the trick won't work.

What's Really Happening

Air may appear to be flimsy stuff, but like all matter, air does have weight. The secret of this trick is that the weight of air presses on all surfaces.

Air envelops the earth in a layer that is thickest at sea level and gets thinner and thinner as you move higher. Most of the earth's air is within the first five or six miles above the earth's surface. A one-inch-square column of air five or six miles high from sea level weighs about 15 pounds. A sheet of newspaper 30 inches long by 22 inches wide has an area of 660 square inches. If 15 pounds are pressing on each of these 660 square inches, the total weight on the newspaper is 660 times 15 pounds, or 9,900 pounds! That'll hold the slat in place, for sure.

Naturally, this kind of weight is also pressing on you. You don't feel the air pressure because the pressure inside your body is the same as outside. They cancel each other out. The same thing is true of air pressure on both sides of a sheet of newspaper. When you smooth the newspaper on the table, you squeeze out most of the air under the paper. The air pressure on top is enough to hold the slat in place if you move fast enough to break the slat before air rushes under the paper.

★
THE CLINGING CUP: SUPPORT BY AIR PRESSURE

You place your left hand on the bottom of a teacup, mutter a few magic words while massaging the back of your hand, and—lo and behold—as you raise your hand, the cup clings! The closest inspection cannot reveal a trace of sticky stuff.

The Setup and the Act

The only prop you need for this trick is a teacup that has a shallow, circular, bowl-shaped hollow bottom. The size of the hollow bottom should be considerably smaller than the palm of your hand: two inches is about right. The cup should not be too heavy, and the bottom should be fairly smooth.

Announce that you have magical powers over the teacup. Place the cup upside down on a table and stand before it. Make a motion as if you are pushing up your sleeves as you get ready to perform. Then moisten the fingertips of your right hand with your tongue (the way you would moisten your finger to turn a page) and brush your hands together so your left palm becomes moist. Do this several times while you talk about how difficult it is to communicate with a cup.

Place your moist left palm firmly on the bottom of the cup. Start rubbing the back of your left hand with the palm of your right. The idea here is to apply enough force to the palm of your left hand to push out the air. If you lean forward slightly as you rub (to add some of the weight of your body), no one will notice the pressure you are applying to the left hand.

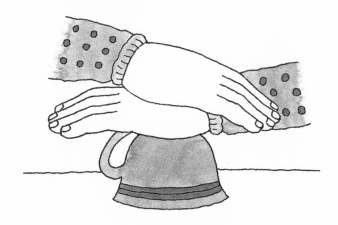

If you have a proper seal, the cup will stick to your hand. You can raise your hand with the cup clinging to it, turn it over, and wave the cup in the air. The suction will not hold very long, though. Practice beforehand so you have an idea of how long the cup will stick. During your performance, release the cup with your right hand before the seal breaks.

After you release the cup, give it to your audience for their examination.

Performance Tips: This trick is for a show with a small audience. Don't be afraid to ham it up. It's also fun to perform informally after dinner. It is, however, one trick that must be practiced until you get the feel of it.

What's Really Happening

A suction cup is a bowl made of rubber that can be used to pick up objects. When the shallow bowl is flattened against a surface, air is forced out of the bowl. When the cup is allowed to return to its regular shape, there is less air inside the cup next to the surface. Such a space, where some air has been removed, is called a *partial vacuum.* A suction cup sticks to the surface because the air pressure outside is greater than the air pressure in the partial vacuum.

In this trick, you create a partial vacuum between your palm and the bottom of the cup by pressing out the air. Moisture on your palm fills in the spaces of the irregular surface of your hand to make an airtight seal. A moist palm is essential to the success of this trick, as it prevents air from leaking in.

★
GATHERING WATERS:
ABOUT VACUUM CLEANING

You challenge your friends to rescue a coin lying in a thin layer of water without wetting their fingers. The water may not be poured off the coin nor tilted away from it. Would you believe the tools for saving this money are a match, a birthday candle, and a glass?

The Setup and the Act

☆ a shallow dish (such as a glass pie pan)
☆ a small piece of modeling clay to act as a candleholder
☆ a birthday candle
☆ a coin
☆ water
☆ red or blue food coloring
☆ matches
☆ an 8-ounce glass

◦ **Since you will be using matches, check with an adult before you do this trick.** Set this trick up right in front of your audience. Make a candleholder out of clay an inch or so off the center of the dish.

Place the coin in the dish near the edge and pour in enough water to completely cover the coin. Add a few drops of food coloring to make the water more visible. Challenge anyone to remove the coin with their fingers without tilting the dish, pouring out the water, or getting their fingers wet.

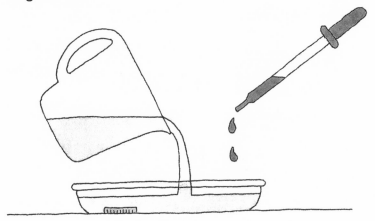

When your audience has run out of ideas, announce that you will accomplish this feat with the aid of a candle, a match, and a glass. Place the candle in the holder. Light the candle. Cover the lit candle with the glass.

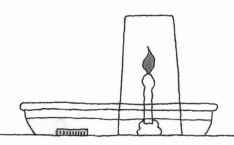

When the candle goes out, the water will rise up into the glass, leaving the coin high and dry. You simply reach in and pick up the coin.

Performance Tips: This effect is good for a small show. You might ask if anyone knows what makes it work. Then explain it. It's a fun science lesson.

What's Really Happening

Scientists aren't completely sure of the whole story. Several things are going on at once here. When a candle burns, it uses oxygen, which makes up about 20 percent of the gases in the air. (Most of the rest of air is another gas called nitrogen.) The flame goes out when all the oxygen has been used. The air pressure inside the glass is now a partial vacuum and is less than the air pressure outside. So the outside air pushes the water up into the glass. At the same time, the flame produces carbon dioxide and heats the air in the glass. Both of these increase the air pressure in the glass, so the rising water takes up less than the 20 percent of space you might expect when the oxygen is used up.

A vacuum cleaner works in much the same way. The motor on a vacuum cleaner makes a partial vacuum inside the vacuum cleaner bag. Outside air pressure makes air rush into this vacuum, sweeping up any small things, like dust, in its path.

★
DRAG RACE:
AERODYNAMIC ACTION

The challenge is to drop a stamp and a fifty-cent piece at the same instant from the same height and have them reach the ground at the same time. Those who try are doomed to fail. Then you, the natural wonder, show how it's done.

The Setup and the Act

All you need is a fifty-cent piece and a stamp that is smaller than the coin. Most people will respond to your challenge by holding the stamp in one hand and the coin in the other. The coin will always reach the ground first.

After a few people have failed, you show how it's done. Place the stamp on top of the coin, making sure there are no corners sticking out over the edge. Press the stamp down to make sure there is as much contact between the two surfaces as possible. The idea is to keep air from moving under the stamp and lifting it from the coin. Drop the coin and stamp together as shown in the picture. Yes, they arrive together on the ground.

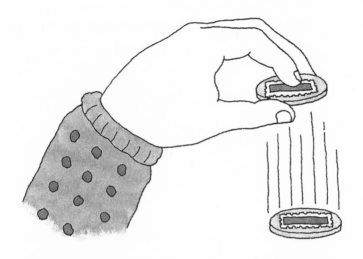

What's Really Happening

Every object moving through air sets up a distur-
bance called *turbulence*. If there is enough turbulence, the flight of the object is unsteady. Air also
exerts friction on objects moving through it. This
force is called air resistance, or *drag*. The amount
of drag on an object and the steadiness of its flight
depend on the shape of the object and its speed.
Streamlining and smoother surfaces reduce drag
and turbulence.

A postage stamp flutters slowly to the ground because drag and turbulence act against the force of gravity. Drag and turbulence also affect a falling coin. But the weight of the coin counteracts them, so the coin is hardly slowed down. When you put the stamp closely on top of the coin, the coin "runs interference" for the stamp and there is little effect of aerodynamics on the stamp.

Of course, if you dropped the coin and stamp from each hand on the moon, where there is no air, they would both hit the ground at the same time!

★
LEAKPROOF STRAINER: A STUDY OF SURFACE TENSION

You pour water through a tea strainer so no one doubts it's full of holes. Then you show how it holds water without spilling a drop. Suddenly either the strainer is leakproof or you've found an invisible lining.

The Setup and the Act

☆   white paraffin (the kind used to seal

jelly jars, which you can get at a super-
market)
☆ an aluminum pan
☆ a wire tea strainer

**Since you will be using the stove, check
with an adult before you begin.** Melt the paraffin in the pan, following the directions on the package. Dip the strainer into the melted wax. As you
remove the strainer, give it a hard shake over the
pan while the paraffin is still hot. The idea is to
coat the wires of the strainer lightly with wax
but still keep it full of holes.

For your act have on the table:

☆ the waxed tea strainer
☆ a pitcher of water
☆ a basin
☆ a small square of plastic wrap that
neatly fits into the tea strainer

Demonstrate that the strainer is full of holes
by pouring water through it into the basin. The
weight of the falling water will force it through
the coated holes.

Then slip the small square of plastic wrap into the strainer as you announce that your magic can keep water in the strainer despite the holes. If anyone comments on the plastic wrap, carry on as if you didn't hear. Let people think you are very bad at making concealed motions.

Pour water into the plastic-lined strainer. Then say, "Oh, you think that the plastic wrap is keeping in the water?" Slide out the plastic and, amazingly, the water remains in the strainer in spite of the holes!

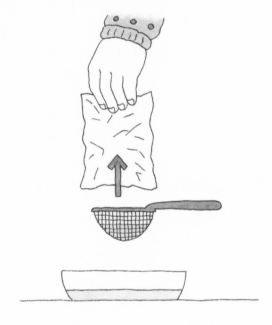

Performance Tips: This is an effective trick for a small audience. Since your props are small, your audience should have a fairly close view. On the other hand, you don't want anyone close enough to detect the way you've "doctored" the strainer.

What's Really Happening

Water is made up of many very tiny particles called *molecules*. When water is a liquid, the molecules are free to move past each other, but they are close enough to be strongly attracted to each other. At the surface, where air and water meet, the attraction between water molecules is the strongest. Water molecules pull together, forming an invisible "skin." This pulling together of the molecules is called *surface tension*.

Surface tension is not a very strong force. Water molecules often come in contact with materials that attract them more than they are attracted to each other. When water is attracted to another surface, that surface becomes wet. When the wetting attraction is strong, surface tension is decreased. On the other hand, if you decrease the wetting attraction, the surface tension is increased. Normally water will wet the wires of a strainer. But water is not attracted to paraffin. Water rolls off a waxed surface. By coating the wires with wax, you prevent them from becoming wet. This increases the surface tension of the water in the holes of the strainer.

The force of <u>falling</u> water is enough to cause water to pass through the waxed holes. The piece of plastic breaks the force of falling water while you are pouring. But when you remove the plastic, the surface tension of the <u>resting</u> water is strong enough to keep it in the strainer.

★
PLAYING MOSES: BREAKING SURFACE TENSION

Moses raised his hands and the Red Sea waters rushed away. You too can make red waters part, leaving a dry spot behind. Behold!

The Setup and the Act

- ☆ water
- ☆ a small flat plate (preferably light in color)
- ☆ red food coloring
- ☆ a straw or medicine dropper
- ☀ ☆ a small bottle of rubbing alcohol that can be disguised as a bottle of "magic fluid"

Pour a thin layer of water into the plate as you talk about the way Moses parted the Red Sea so his people could escape the Egyptian soldiers. Add a few drops of red food coloring to make the water truly a "Red Sea."

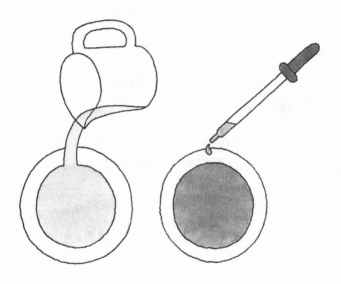

Now explain that you have a magic fluid that can do what Moses did. Put the straw into the bottle of alcohol. The alcohol fills the straw up to the level of its surface. Put your finger over the open top of the straw. **(Do not put the straw in your mouth.)** Lift out the straw, keeping your finger in place. As long as you cover the top of the straw, the alcohol will not run out. Place the end of the straw over the center of the red water. Lift up your finger so the alcohol runs out onto the plate. When it hits the surface, the red water rushes away, leaving a dry spot where you put the alcohol.

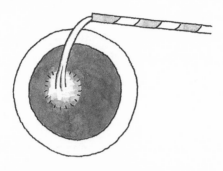

Performance Tips: This trick has to be viewed up close by a small audience. If you want to do an effective demonstration for your class, use an overhead projector. Use a large glass baking dish on the projector surface instead of a plate.

What's Really Happening

Different liquids have different surface tensions. See for yourself. Put drops of water, salad oil, rubbing alcohol ☠, and turpentine ☠ on a sheet of waxed paper. Compare the shapes of the drops by looking at them sideways. The highest, roundest drop has the most surface tension, while the flattest drop has the least.

When liquids with different surface tensions come into contact with each other, there is a lot of motion. The two liquids will pull in opposite directions, and the liquid with the stronger surface tension will pull harder. If the pull is strong enough and the depth of the liquid is very shallow, such a tug-of-war between two liquids leaves a dry spot. In this trick, the surface tension of water is stronger than that of alcohol, so it wins the war until the two liquids mix and flow over the dry spot.

★
INTELLIGENT EGGS: BUOYANCY

You give two eggs to a member of your audience and ask him or her to write the word "sink" on one egg and "float" on the other. You then place each egg in a glass of water and order both of them to obey the commands written on them. Naturally, they're smart enough to do as they are told.

The Setup and the Act

- ☆ two 8-ounce glasses
- ☆ water
- ☆ 4 tablespoons sugar
- ☆ two uncooked eggs
- ☆ a laundry marking pencil

Well before performance time, fill the glasses with water to about ¾ inch below the top. Dissolve the sugar in one glass. Be sure to remember by position which glass is which.

Announce that you have two intelligent eggs that obey written commands. Have a member of your audience label them with the words "sink" and "float."

When the marked eggs are returned to you, put the egg marked "sink" in the glass with plain water and the "float" egg in the sugar water. Amaz-

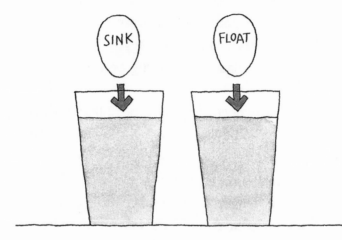

ing, but they obey their commands. Afterward, you can break open the eggs to show that there is no trick inside.

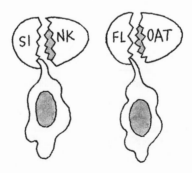

Performance Tips: This trick uses an old standby of magicians called "misdirection." You call attention to the eggs, making it appear that any difference in behavior is due to them. This diverts people's attention away from where the real secret of the trick lies.

This is an effective trick for a small magic show.

What's Really Happening

When you put a body (such as your own) into water, here's what happens: Water is pushed aside as your body takes up space that had been occupied by water. If the body could be attached to a scale, you'd find that it weighed less in water than it weighed on land. A floating body would register zero on a scale. That's because water exerts an upward force, called *buoyancy*, that works against gravity.

Some liquids have greater buoyancy than others. If you've ever gone swimming in salt water, you've probably noticed that you float more easily than you do in swimming-pool water. In this trick, you used sugar dissolved in water instead of salt. Solutions of sugar or salt have a greater buoyant force than plain water. You might want to experiment with salt water. I found sugar worked better, but you might find otherwise.

★

RISING RAISINS: BUOYANCY AND SURFACE TENSION

Drop a few raisins in some ginger ale, and they quickly sink to the bottom of the glass. But, at the sound of your masterful voice, some rise to the surface, only to fall back again at your command. Directions for training raisins follow.

The Setup and the Act

☆   a few raisins
☆   a glass of fresh ginger ale or other light-colored soda

Drop a few raisins into the soda. Mention that some raisins are more obedient than others. Watch carefully as bubbles collect on the raisins' surfaces. It will take a few seconds for the raisins to start to rise. As soon as you see one of the raisins beginning to move, command it to rise. When it reaches the surface, tell it to fall.

Performance Tips: This trick has to be seen close up. It's most effective if done when you're sitting around with a few friends having a snack. If you handle the commands with confidence, some people won't realize that they have nothing to do with the rise and fall of raisins.

What's Really Happening

There are several things going on here. Soda contains carbon dioxide gas, which rises to the surface as bubbles. Bubbles rise because the buoyant force of the soda liquid is greater than the weight of a bubble. The rough surface of a raisin provides many points of attachment for gas bubbles. When enough bubbles collect on a raisin's surface, it becomes buoyant enough to rise to the top.

The gas inside a bubble expands as the bubble moves up to the surface and the pressure of the liquid on it decreases. At the surface, the bubble expands even more, and the surface tension of its liquid wall breaks, releasing the gas to the air. When the bubbles break, the raisin loses its buoyant support and sinks back to the bottom, where it remains until a new batch of bubbles collects on its surface.

☆　　☆　　☆

★
DIVING DOLL:
HYDRAULIC PRESSURE
AND BUOYANCY

With a flourish, you bring forward a tiny doll floating
in a baby bottle full of water. The doll sinks and
rises at the command of your audience.

The Setup

☆ water
☆ a bowl
☆ a large nail
☆ a pair of pliers
☆ an inexpensive, hollow plastic toy doll,
about two inches long, small enough
to fit into the bottle (You can get
dolls like this in dime stores and nov-
elty shops. They are made in a single
piece, without movable arms or legs.)
☆ some small lead fishing weights
☆ a clear 8-ounce plastic baby bottle
☆ a blind nipple (This is a nipple that
has no holes. It can be purchased at
any drugstore.)
☆ plastic wrap

The doll may come wrapped in a small piece of flannel. Remove this. Fill the bowl with cold water and set it aside. Use the nail to make a hole in the feet of the doll. **You will be using the stove to heat the nail, so check with an adult before you begin.** Hold the head end of the nail with the pliers. Heat the pointed end over the burner of the stove.

Press the hot point of the nail into the bottom of the doll's feet. Make one hole just large enough to insert two or three small lead fishing weights. Using the pliers, drop the nail into the bowl of water to cool it.

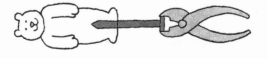

It takes a bit of fussing to get the doll diver to work properly. Put a small amount of water in the doll.

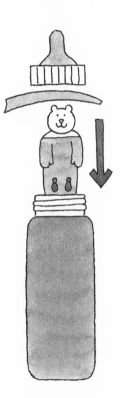

Drop it, feet first, into the baby bottle filled with water. The doll should rise and come to rest with its head just touching the surface. If the doll remains near the bottom of the bottle, remove it and shake out some of the water. If the doll floats above the surface, remove it and add a little water.

When the doll is resting in the proper position, place a small piece of plastic wrap over the mouth of the bottle and screw on the top with the blind nipple in place. The seal must be airtight. You may find that the doll sinks a bit when you screw on the top. If this happens, take the whole thing apart and remove some of the water from the doll. It should maintain the proper position with the top screwed in place. It's working properly when you squeeze the sides of the bottle slightly and the doll sinks to the bottom.

Note: A medicine dropper with a rubber bulb may be substituted for the doll. You'll have to play with it to see how much water you need to put in the dropper to make it rise and fall. Some people paint a face on the medicine dropper.

The Act

Show your doll diver to the audience. Have them command the doll to sink. Squeeze the sides of the bottle gently to send the doll to the bottom, and release the pressure when your audience commands the doll to rise. No one should be able to detect the small motion of your hand.

Performance Tips: You may want to pass the bottle around so others can try and make the doll sink and rise. You may wish to explain the science behind the trick.

What's Really Happening

The doll has an air bubble in its head, which makes it buoyant enough to float just under the surface of the water in the bottle. The water in the doll can flow freely in and out through the hole in the bottom of the doll's feet.

When you squeeze the sides of the bottle, you apply pressure to the water, forcing the water up through the hole in the doll's feet. The air bubble gets smaller and the additional water inside the doll makes it less buoyant, so it sinks. When you release the pressure, the air bubble springs back to its former size, pushing out the extra water, and the doll is again able to rise to the surface.

Pressure that travels through a liquid is called *hydraulic pressure*. Hydraulic pressure travels through the water and squeezes the gas into a smaller space. This trick is a variation on a classic physical phenomenon called a *Cartesian diver*.

ENERGY
ENCHANTMENTS

What do heat, light, electricity, and motion have in common? They are all forms of *energy*—which along with matter makes up the universe. The only way we know that energy exists is from the way it acts on matter. We see light and hear sound from the way our eyes and ears react to light and sound. Energy makes a car move, a light bulb turn on, and a flower grow.

One kind of energy can change into another. Rub your hands together and you change motion into heat. Power plants change the energy of falling water or burning fuel into electricity. A bow drawn across a violin string changes the motion of the bow into sound.

The tricks in this chapter will reveal some charming things about energy that will enchant your audiences.

★
THE WRITHING SNAKE:
KINETIC AND POTENTIAL ENERGY

From your pocket you produce a small coiled "snake" that twists and writhes as if it were alive.

The Setup and the Act

☆ a 4-inch piece of stretchable plastic wrap
☆ a paper clip

Hold one corner of the plastic wrap in one hand. Twist the wrap with the other hand by making circular motions with your index finger.

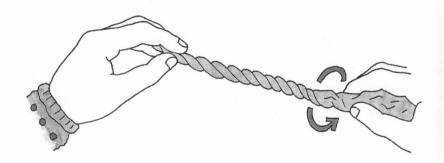

Continue until the plastic wrap is <u>very</u> tightly wound in a rope shape. Then coil it so it is flat and round. Make a small knot at one end (being careful not to let it unwind) to be the snake's head. Hold the coil in position with a paper clip and keep it in a pocket until you are ready to perform.

Announce that you have a live act as you pull out the "snake." Remove the paper clip while your hand is still hidden from sight, holding the snake so that it doesn't unwind. Bring out the coiled snake and release it.

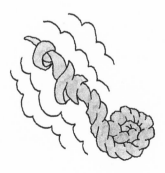

Performance Tips: This is amusing for a close-up audience, especially one with young children. Produce the snake quickly to add a surprise factor.

What's Really Happening

Moving things have *kinetic* energy, which means "energy of motion." In this trick, the kinetic energy of your hands twists the plastic wrap. The twisted plastic wrap stores this energy, much as a tightly wound spring stores energy. Stored energy is called *potential* energy. When you release the wrap, the potential energy changes back into the kinetic energy of your writhing snake.

★
THE DEVIL'S HANDKERCHIEF: HEAT CONDUCTION

You hold the red-hot end of a glowing piece of wood against a handkerchief for fifteen seconds. Amazingly, the handkerchief isn't even scorched.

The Setup and the Act

☆ a handkerchief
☆ a quarter

☆   a candle

☆   matches

☆   a pencil or a small wooden stick

♦ **Since you will be using fire, check with an adult before you begin.** Wrap the handkerchief around the quarter, twisting it behind the coin to make a flat surface. Set the coin and

handkerchief aside. Light the candle. Put one end of the wooden stick in the flame and keep it there until at least a quarter of an inch is glowing red-hot. Hold the glowing end against the cloth lying flat on the coin for about fifteen seconds. Remove the wood and unwrap the quarter. Show both sides of the handkerchief to your audience with a flourish. You'll find no trace of scorched fabric.

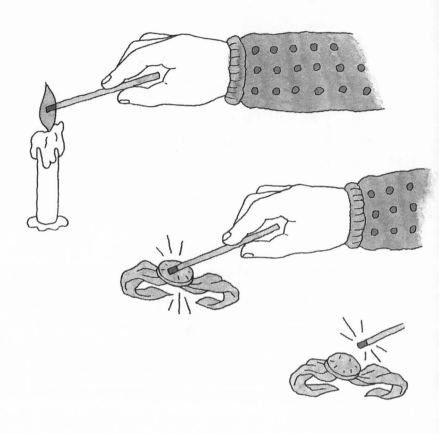

Performance Tips: This effect has to be viewed close up. If you would like to turn it into a science demonstration (and don't mind burning a hole in the fabric), try it again without the coin. It will take only about fifteen seconds to burn a hole in the cloth.

What's Really Happening

Fire is a release of heat and light energy when a fuel combines with oxygen in the air. To start a fire, you need fuel, oxygen, and a source of heat. Some fuels need less heat to start burning than others. For example, a match head starts burning from the small amount of heat generated by friction when you strike the match. A handkerchief starts burning at a much higher temperature.

In this trick, you prevented the cloth from scorching by removing the heat from the cloth before it got hot enough to burn. The heat from the glowing wood passed through the cloth into the quarter, which is a *heat conductor.* A heat conductor gets hot very quickly and easily without itself burning. Heat travels through the quarter, leaving the area being heated so the handkerchief cannot build up enough heat to burn. Metals are good heat conductors, and silver and copper, of which the quarter is made, are among the best. If you feel the quarter right after removing the heat source, it will be evenly warm all over. The part that was directly against the heat source won't be any warmer than the rest of the coin.

★
A STAMPED-OUT STAMP: LIGHT REFRACTION

You place a perfectly transparent object over a postage stamp and the stamp disappears! You've used a "no-looking" glass for this stamp act.

The Setup and the Act

- ☆ an empty peanut-butter jar and lid
- ☆ water
- ☆ a postage stamp

You can paint and decorate the lid of the jar with nail polish, if you wish. Fill the jar with water and screw on the top.

Show your audience the covered jar, pointing out that it is transparent and easily seen through. Place the jar over the stamp. If it is correctly placed, no one can see the stamp from any angle around the jar. Remove the jar and the stamp is still there.

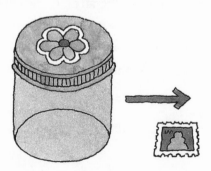

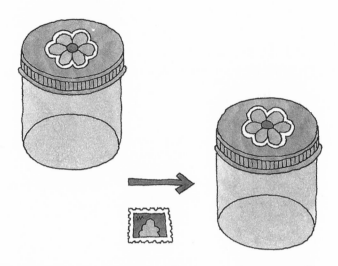

Performance Tips: This is a close-up effect. You must be careful to fill the jar, because if it is less than full, the stamp will appear to be inside the jar.

What's Really Happening

Light is a form of energy that travels at very high speeds through space, air, water, glass, and many other materials. However, light travels at different speeds through different transparent materials. At a boundary between water and glass, two transparent materials, the light changes speed and is bent, or *refracted*.

In this trick, the lid of the jar prevents you from looking directly down on the stamp, and you must look at it at an angle through the side of the jar. As light from the stamp passes from the water to the glass to the air, it is bent in such a way that the stamp looks like it's higher than it really is. If you fill the jar with water, the image of the stamp will be so high that you cannot see it from the side.

Variety Act

A curved transparent object can act as a lens and bend light so that the image is reversed. The picture shows how this happens. Place a card with an arrow drawn on it behind your water-filled peanut butter jar. When you look at it through the jar, the direction of the arrow will be reversed. You will have to experiment to see how far behind the jar you must place the card to get the proper effect.

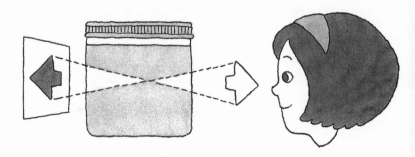

★

THE PHANTOM MEMORY: PHOSPHORESCENCE

A friend secretly selects a number on a chart by covering it with a small piece of cardboard. You see nothing, yet you can later tell where the cardboard rested.

The Setup

☆ phosphorescent tape (This is sometimes called *luminous tape.* It's available at hardware stores and is used to mark light switches, etc., so they are visible in the dark.)

☆ colored paper

☆ a marking pen

☆ scissors

☆ a small piece of cardboard

☆ a dark scarf or a large piece of dark cloth

☆ pencil and paper

Put several strips of luminous tape on colored paper and mark the strips off in numbered squares of the same size, as shown in the picture. Outline the squares in ink. Cut a piece of cardboard to exactly fit one square. To perform, you'll need the chart, the cardboard, the scarf, and the pencil and paper.

 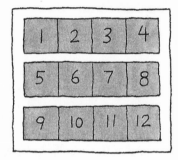

The Act

This trick must be performed in a brightly lit room. A tabletop with a lamp on it is a good place on which to rest the number chart.

Place the dark scarf over your head so it covers your face. With your back turned, ask a friend to secretly select a number by covering it with the cardboard square.

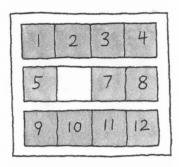

Now you have to stall for time. Ask your friend to do some math with the number he or she selected. The pencil and paper are for figuring. You might ask that the number be multiplied by five, that the year of your friend's birth be added, today's date be subtracted, and so on. Most people won't realize that this is a lot of nonsense.

Ask for the solution to the math, have the scratch paper torn up, and have the cardboard square removed from the chart. Point out that there is no evidence to give you a clue to the selected number. Pick up the chart, turn your back again, and bring the chart up under the scarf. (You can claim to be tuning in to your thought waves.) In the dim light under the scarf you'll see that the square that was covered is not as bright as the others. Announce the correct number with a flourish.

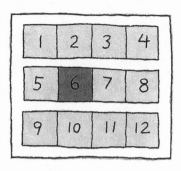

Performance Tips: This is a good trick for a show with a small audience so everyone can get a close-up look at the chart. If you repeat the trick, use an entirely different set of mathematical operations that will thoroughly confuse everyone.

What's Really Happening

Some minerals have the unusual ability of absorbing light energy, which they can later release as ghostly green light you can see in the dark. This ability is called *phosphorescence.* The brightness of the glow depends on the amount of light the phosphorescent material has been exposed to. If there has been a long exposure to bright light, the material will glow more brightly in the dark than when there has been a shorter exposure. By covering a square with cardboard, you've limited the amount of exposure of that square. Thus, you appear to be pretty bright yourself!

★
A SONG-AND-DANCE ACT: SYMPATHETIC VIBRATIONS

You run your finger around the rim of a crystal goblet, making it sing. Meanwhile, a wire on a nearby goblet dances.

The Setup

☆ two identical crystal goblets with stems
☆ a straightened paper clip or hairpin
☆ water

This trick takes a bit of fussing and practice before you'll be ready to perform. First practice making a goblet sing. The glass and your finger should be clean and free of grease. Moisten the forefinger of one hand. Hold the base of the glass in place with the other hand as you rotate your wet finger around the rim. You'll soon learn just how much pressure to apply to produce a steady ringing tone.

The next problem is to get both goblets to produce the same tone. To tune the goblets, tap the sides, first of one, then of the other with a wooden pencil. This lets you test the tone. Between tests, add a small amount of water to one or the other goblet until they produce the same note. Adding water lowers the tone and removing it raises the tone. The trick will not work if the goblets are not properly tuned.

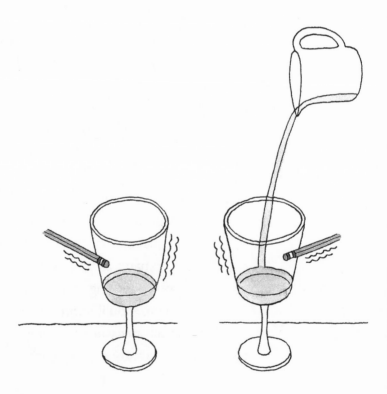

The Act

Announce that two friendly glasses will perform a song-and-dance act. The goblets should be side by side about two inches apart. The wire hairpin or opened paper clip should be lying across the rim of one goblet. Run your wet finger around the rim of the other goblet, making it sing. Its tone will have an effect on the other goblet, causing the wire to dance around on the rim.

What's Really Happening

Sound is produced in air by vibrating objects, such as a plucked guitar string, a struck bell, or air rushing over your vocal cords.

When you wet your finger and run it around the rim of a crystal goblet, you set up vibrations that sound like a pure tone, which is the simplest kind of sound energy. The highness or lowness of the tone depends on the number of vibrations per second. If a nearby goblet is tuned to the same tone as the goblet that's vibrating, it will respond by vibrating when the tone is produced. Sometimes such *sympathetic vibrations* can be so strong that the object breaks. An example is the breaking of a glass by an opera singer's sustained note.

In this trick, the vibrations of one goblet set up sympathetic vibrations in another one nearby. You won't, however, produce a strong enough tone to break the other glass.

★
THE WONDROUS WAND: ELECTROSTATICS

With a wave of your wand you make paper dance, move a plastic bubble, and wiggle some toothpicks.

Both you and your audience can get a charge from this.

The Setup and the Act

☆ a plastic rod or tube for a wand (I used the handle of a clean plastic fly-swatter)
☆ a wool scarf
☆ various items to be "electrified," such as: plastic tinsel, plastic bubbles (the kind you blow on the end of a straw from liquid that comes in a tube), wooden toothpicks, paper people cut out of tissue paper and placed in a glass dish covered with plastic wrap

Have everything ready before you perform. Show your friends your "magic" wand. Rub it well with the scarf.

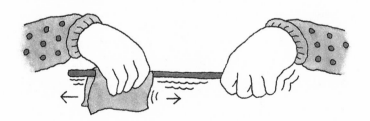

Wave the charged wand near the objects to be "electrified." The objects will move as the wand comes near them. Rub the wand whenever you find it needs recharging.

Performance Tips: It's better if you perform this trick on a dry day, as moisture in the air prevents a good charge from building up. Experiment to see what effect the charged wand has when you bring it near another object and when you touch it to that object.

What's Really Happening

Thousands of years ago the Greeks knew of a "magic" stone—a kind of petrified pine resin known today as amber. When amber is rubbed with fur, it gets a strange temporary power. Nearby bits of paper and cork move toward the stone and stick to it. The Greek name for amber is *elektros*. Today this power is called *electrostatic attraction*.

You produce electrostatic attraction in many nonmetals by rubbing them with other materials. In this trick you rub plastic with wool and give the plastic (and the wool) an electric charge, which gives them the power to attract other objects. A charged object acts something like a magnet for a short time, until it loses its charge to the air or to the objects it is touching.

Variety Acts

Charge yourself by walking across a woolen rug while wearing rubber-soled shoes. The charge in your hands can be transferred to a playing card you are holding. Slap the charged playing card against the wall, and electrostatic attraction will hold it there for a few minutes.

★

Open a single sheet of newspaper, hold it up against the wall, and rub it with a woolen cloth. When you remove the cloth, the newspaper will cling to the wall due to electrostatic attraction.

CHEMICAL CONJURING

Rub a stick against a surface and it bursts into flames. Magic? No, chemistry. A match is coated with a material that burns when friction adds a little heat. Burning is one of many chemical reactions.

Modern chemistry is the science that deals with the properties of materials and how materials can be transformed. Often the products of chemical reactions are very different from the original materials. For example, two colorless gases, oxygen and hydrogen, combine explosively to form water, a colorless liquid.

You can use some chemistry as a part of your act. Discover how science truly can be magic.

★
THE FLYING FLAME: INTRODUCING A CHEMICAL REACTION

You make a flame jump from one candle to another. And, in a variety act, you separate a flame from a candle so it burns a few inches <u>above</u> the wick.

The Setup and the Act

☆ waxed paper
☆ two long dinner candles
☆ matches

♦ **Since you will be using fire, check with an adult before you begin.** Spread the waxed paper on the table to catch candle wax as it drips. Light both candles, announcing that you have the power to make a flame jump from one to the other.

Hold a candle in each hand. When the flames are burning strongly, turn the candles sideways so they are burning near each other. Blow out the flame of one candle and move it an inch or two below the other, still burning, candle. The column of smoke from the unlit candle should rise to meet the flame. The reaction quickly travels down the smoke, causing the wick to ignite again. Fire appears to jump through the air.

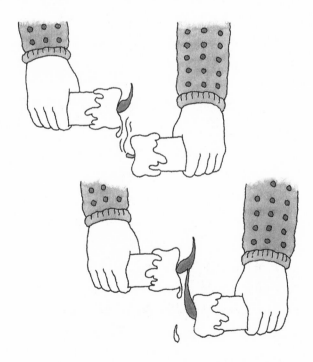

Performance Tips: This effect has to be viewed up close. Also, it won't work well if the room is drafty.

What's Really Happening

Burning is one of the most familiar of all chemical reactions. Hot candle wax reacts with oxygen in the air to form water vapor and carbon dioxide. The wax seems to disappear as a candle burns, but it is only transformed into the two products water vapor and carbon dioxide, which disappear into the air.

All chemical reactions involve energy. In this case, you see heat and light energy given off in a flame during the reaction. The match needed to ignite the candle supplies enough energy to make the wax hot enough to combine with oxygen. After that, the heat given off by the reaction is enough to keep it going so that additional wax reacts.

When you blow out a candle, some of the hot wax leaves the wick as smoke. This wax vapor is hot enough to burn if you bring a flame close to it. The flame travels down the column of hot-wax vapor to reignite the wick from which the vapor comes. So it appears as if the flame is jumping through the air.

Variety Act

You will need:

- ☆ a small jar
- ☆ measuring spoons
- ☆ vinegar
- ☆ baking soda
- ☆ a small birthday candle in a wire holder that you can make from a paper clip (see illustration)
- ☆ matches

❖ **Since you will be using fire, check with an adult before performing this trick.** Put about two tablespoons of vinegar and one tablespoon of baking soda in the bottom of a small jar. The bubbles that form contain carbon dioxide gas. Carbon dioxide is heavier than air, and it drives air from the jar as it collects. (You can also collect a jar of carbon dioxide, as suggested in the next trick.)

Light the candle. When it is burning strongly,

lower it carefully by the wire holder into the jar of carbon dioxide. When the top of the candle goes into the jar, the flame will remain near the mouth of the jar while the candle wick is extinguished. It will take a bit of experimenting to see how far you can lower the candle before the flame goes out.

Carbon dioxide gas does not support burning. In this variety act you take advantage of this property. When you lower the burning candle into the carbon dioxide, the flame at the candle wick is extinguished. The column of wax vapor continues to rise, however, and it feeds the flame that remains behind at the boundary of the carbon dioxide and the oxygen in the air.

★
THE SPIRITED
FIRE EXTINGUISHER:
CARBON DIOXIDE IN ACTION

You pick up an empty jar, empty its invisible contents over a candle, and the flame goes out! Are you pouring it on or putting it on? Let them wonder.

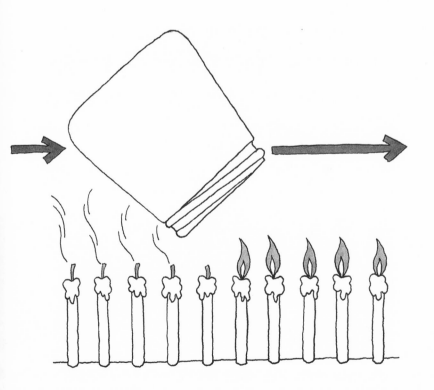

The Setup

- ☆ several jars of carbon dioxide (see the procedure below for collecting carbon dioxide)
- ☆ a candleholder with candles (you can make a long candleholder out of modeling clay and put in a row of ten or fifteen birthday candles)
- ☆ matches

To collect carbon dioxide:

- ☆ a jar (large peanut-butter size) with lid
- ☆ a screwdriver
- ☆ modeling clay
- ☆ plastic tubing (this can be obtained from a store that sells aquarium supplies)
- ☆ jars with lids to hold gas
- ☆ a pan of water
- ☆ a bottle of club soda
- ☆ a bowl of warm water
- ☆ a plate

Poke a hole in the lid of the large jar with the screwdriver. This jar will be used as a gas generating chamber.

Put one end of the plastic tubing through the hole and mold clay around it to make an airtight seal with the lid. Fill one of the collecting jars with water. Submerge it in the pan of water and turn it upside down. Leave it sitting on the bottom. Fill the generating chamber half full of club soda. Screw on the top and pass the tube into the pan. Put the generating chamber in a bowl of warm water. As its contents heat up, carbon dioxide gas (the fizz in soda) is driven off. You'll see bubbles coming out of the end of the tube in the pan. Let the gas bubble for a few minutes to drive out the air in the generating chamber. Then put the end of the tube in the upside-down jar in the pan.

Carbon dioxide bubbles rise and fill the jar, driving out the water. You can easily see when the jar is full of gas. Remove the jar of carbon dioxide by sliding a plate under it while it is still in the water. After taking the jar out of the water, turn it right side up, remove the plate, and screw on a cover until you are ready to perform. Continue with another jar, and perhaps another. You'll know when all the carbon dioxide has been driven out of the soda when no more bubbles come out the end of the tube.

Before performing, have the jars of gas ready and have the candles and matches handy. There should be no sign of the equipment used to collect the gas.

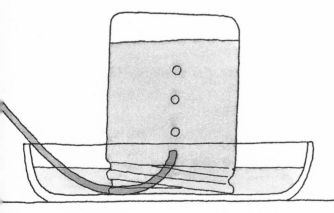

The Act

♦ **Since you will be using fire, check with an adult before you begin.** Pass a closed jar of carbon dioxide around so all can see it is empty. (Don't let anyone open it.) Tell the audience you can put out candles with the help of a "spirit" trapped in the seemingly empty jars. Light the candles. Remove the cover of a jar and make a pouring motion over the candles. They will all go out. If people want to see the trick again, you can repeat it with another jar of gas.

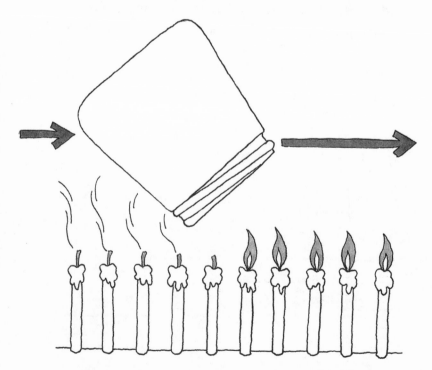

What's Really Happening

Carbon dioxide is hard to detect because it is a colorless, odorless gas. Air is a mixture of colorless, odorless gases, mainly oxygen and nitrogen. Unlike oxygen, however, carbon dioxide will not react with a fuel and does not support burning. In fact, it can be used to prevent burning. Carbon dioxide is also heavier than air. That's why you can leave an open jar upright for a few minutes without losing the gas and still be able to pour it over a flame.

★
THINK MILK: PRECIPITATION

Water changes into milk as you pour it into a glass. It's thought waves on milk that did it.

The Setup

☗ ☆ photographic fixer, also known as hypo or sodium thiosulfate (you can purchase this very inexpensively at any photography store)

▲ ✗ ☆   liquid bleach <u>containing sodium hypo-</u><u>chlorite</u> (read the label, as this is not ordinary chlorine bleach)
☆   a colorless glass pitcher
☆   a colorless glass tumbler
☆   a pencil to serve as a stirring rod and a wand

Check with an adult before beginning. Mix the hypo according to the directions on the package. You can store what you don't use in a dark bottle with a cap. Be sure to label the bottle.

Put about one cup of hypo into the pitcher and add an equal amount of water.

Put a few drops of bleach on the bottom of the glass so that it is unnoticeable.

Only the pitcher, glass, and wand are present for your performance.

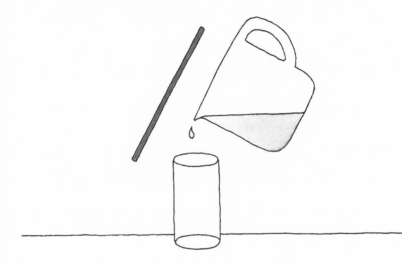

The Act

Tell your audience that you have a pitcher of water. Ask them to name other drinks. Usually someone will say "milk." But if that doesn't happen, you might bring up the subject of milk by saying it is considered to be the perfect food.

Then ask everyone to think hard about milk (or to chant "milk" over and over again) while you pour the "water" into the glass. Use the wand to stir. You might suggest that your magic caused skim milk to form, as the fluid has a watery appearance. Remind them that butterfat in whole milk has too much cholesterol and that skim milk is healthier.

Caution: Don't let anyone drink the solution, as it is poisonous. Pour it down the drain as soon as the trick is finished.

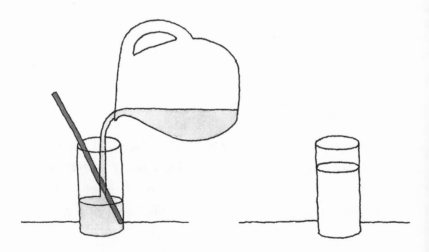

What's Really Happening

Many chemical reactions take place in water solutions. When a substance is in solution, its smallest particles (atoms or molecules) are separated from one another by water molecules. Molecules are much too small to see, so solutions are clear and you can't tell them from plain water by just looking at them.

In this trick you mix two solutions together, and the reaction produces a product that doesn't dissolve in water. It appears as finely divided particles, called a *precipitate*, which gives the mixture a milky appearance.

In this reaction the precipitate is sulfur—one of the 92 natural elements in the earth's crust. Chemists sometimes call this precipitate *milk of sulfur*.

★
THE BLUE FLASHBACK:
A REVERSIBLE REACTION

Pour water into a glass and it changes into ink. Pour the ink into another glass and it changes back into water. Wave your wand and it's ink again.

The Setup

☆ 1 tablespoon starch solution (see the recipe below)

▲ ☢ ☆ ½ cup 3% hydrogen peroxide (you can purchase this at any drugstore)

☆ ½ cup water

☆ 1 tablespoon white vinegar

▲ ☢ ☆ a few drops iodine

☢ ☆ one or two drops hypo (see p. 109)

☆ three colorless glasses

☆ a wand

To make starch solution:

☆ water

☆ a small saucepan

☆ 1 teaspoon cornstarch

☆ a large jar with a lid (has to hold at least 2 cups)

Check with an adult before beginning this trick and before using the stove. Put one cup of water in the saucepan. Add the cornstarch. Heat until the cornstarch is dissolved. Add another cup of water. Store in the jar.

This trick works best when the starch solution is fairly fresh. Put the starch solution, hydrogen peroxide, water, and vinegar in one glass. Put a few drops of iodine on the bottom of another glass. (If the glass has a thick bottom, no one will notice the iodine.) Put one or two drops of hypo on the bottom of the third glass.

Only the three prepared glasses and the wand should be present at the performance.

The Act

A good story for this trick might be one about a secret agent who kept trying to make invisible ink that kept becoming visible.

Hold the glass of clear liquid and call it invisible ink. Pour it into the glass containing iodine. It will turn blue-black.

Then pour it into the glass containing the hypo and give the solution a stir with the wand. It will instantly become colorless again, but within fifteen seconds the color will change back to blue-black.

Performance Tips: If you practice this trick to get the timing right, you can make it look as if a wave of your wand changed the color. This trick is good for a show.

Caution: Don't let anyone drink the solution, as it is poisonous. Pour it down the drain as soon as the trick is finished.

What's Really Happening

Many chemical reactions are reversible. That is, reacting substances form new products, which then break down to re-form the original chemicals. Diluted starch solution looks like plain water. When starch reacts with iodine, it forms a substance that has a blue-black color and looks like ink. Hypo breaks down the starch-iodine product, and the solution becomes clear again. The hypo forms a product with the iodine. Meanwhile, a fourth substance, hydrogen peroxide, is slowly breaking down and giving off tiny bubbles of oxygen. Oxygen reacts with the hypo-iodine product, combining with the hypo. Now the iodine is again free to react with the starch, which is still present, and you've got the ink again. The return of color takes time because the oxygen is being given off slowly. The color change takes place when there is enough iodine released to react with the starch.

Variety Act

You can get the reaction to reverse itself again by adding additional hypo. One way to deliver a few drops of hypo without anyone noticing is to use a wand that has been dipped in hypo. Substitute a spare wand that has been resting in a container of hypo solution.

★
THE PURPLE PALETTE: A CHEMICAL INDICATOR

You bring forth a bottle of purple paint and pour it into three glasses. It instantly changes into pink, green, and yellow paint—a magic way of creating colors.

The Setup

- ☆ red cabbage juice (see procedure below)
- ☆ measuring spoons
- ☆ white vinegar
- ∭ ☓ ▲ ☆ clear (not sudsing) household ammonia
- ☓ ▲ ☆ chlorine bleach
- ☆ three colorless glasses

To prepare red cabbage juice:

- ☆ red cabbage
- ☆ a knife

☆ a stainless steel or enamel pot

☆ water

☆ a strainer

☆ a colorless pitcher or bottle

Check with an adult before you begin this trick and before you use the stove. Cut up the cabbage into many fine pieces and put it in a pot with enough water to cover it. Heat until boiling. Strain the juice into a pitcher or bottle. Add water to fill the bottle if you wish. You can store red cabbage juice covered in the refrigerator for several days. It should be cool before you perform.

Before a performance put about $\frac{1}{2}$ teaspoon of white vinegar in one glass, $\frac{1}{2}$ teaspoon of ammonia in another glass, and $\frac{1}{2}$ teaspoon of bleach in a third glass. It is not likely that your audience will notice such a small amount of liquid at the bottom of each glass, but you can make certain it is unnoticeable by letting it stand or using a hair dryer until the water in each solution evaporates. When you add cabbage juice, the solutions re-form immediately.

The Act

Show your audience a bottle of "paint." You might make up a story about how the purple color can be transformed into other colors if the audience chants the right magic words.

Pour the purple "paint" into each glass. In vinegar it becomes pink. In ammonia it becomes bright green. In chlorine bleach it turns yellow.

Caution: Do not permit anyone to drink the contents of the glasses. Pour them down the drain as soon as the trick is finished.

What's Really Happening

Color changes are one way chemists know when a reaction is taking place. Certain dyes, such as litmus (which chemists use) and red cabbage juice, change color in a predictable way when they come into contact with certain chemicals. One such group, called *acids*, includes vinegar, lemon juice, and sulfuric acid. Acids change litmus from blue to pink and red cabbage juice from purple to pink. Another group, called *bases* or *alkalies*, includes soap, ammonia, lye, and baking soda. Bases change pink litmus to blue and purple cabbage juice to green.

The pigment that makes red cabbage juice purple can also be bleached to make it a pale-yellow color.

You may want to fool around with leftover cabbage juice and see what household products make it change color. You can use it to tell which are acids and which are bases. Just be careful to read the labels, as some household chemicals are poisonous or irritating to the skin.

PERCEPTUAL PUZZLEMENTS

What you see is not always what's really happening. X rays are light you cannot see. There are sounds you cannot hear. And moving pictures are not really moving. A series of still pictures is flashing so quickly before your eyes that the images appear to be moving. There are limits to your senses, and your senses can be fooled.

Science has explored the limits of human senses and the ways our senses can fool us. When our senses are fooled, we experience something called an *illusion*. The word illusion comes from a Latin word meaning "to make fun of," and illusions can be a great part of your magic act.

Here are some illusions for your entertainment.

★
QUICK MONEY:
REACTION TIME

You offer a dollar bill as a prize to anyone who can catch it as you let it fall. Yet time after time, it slips through grasping fingers. No one, it seems, knows how to hang on to money except you.

The Setup and the Act

All you need for this trick is a fairly new and unwrinkled dollar bill. (If you use a five, the trick is even more impressive.)

Announce to your audience that anyone who catches the bill when you let it drop can keep it. Hold the bill vertically by one end. Have a friend put his or her fingers around the bill. Tell the audience this is so your friend will be as "ready as possible" to grab the money as it moves past. Your friend is not to touch the bill until you let go.

Others may want to try after the first person fails. You won't lose the money as long as you follow these directions.

If you drop the bill yourself, you will always be able to catch the money. (So will anyone else who is both dropping and catching.)

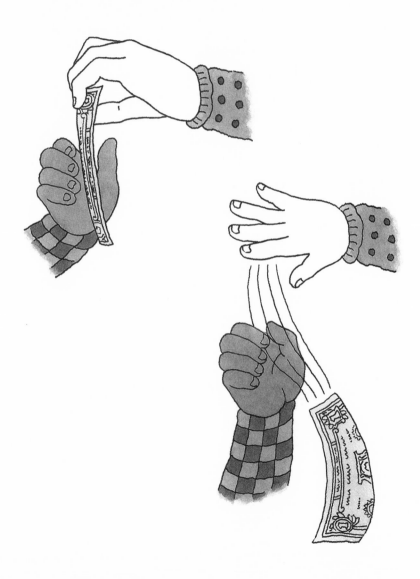

What's Really Happening

It takes a small amount of time—called *reaction time*—to move our muscles in reaction to something we see. The reaction time to respond to the sight of the falling dollar bill is very small, less than ¼ second for most people. But this isn't fast enough. The bill falls past the grasping fingers faster than the reaction time.

When you hold the bill yourself, you are not using the sight of the falling bill as a signal to grasp it. Instead, you are reacting to the internal feeling of letting go with one hand. You can coordinate the grasping motion with this internal muscle signal fast enough to catch the bill.

★
MATTER THROUGH MATTER: A MOTION ILLUSION

With a flick of your finger you make a stick move through a steel bar. There's more to this than meets the eye.

The Setup and the Act

☆ a large safety pin
☆ a 2½-inch stick of wood or plastic (if you use a wooden match, cut off the head)

Insert the pin through the exact center of the stick. Move the stick over to the center of the shaft of the pin. Wiggle the stick around so it moves freely but will hold its position when you stop moving it.

To create the illusion: Hold the head of the pin in one hand. Turn the stick so the top is behind the top shaft of the pin, as the pin faces the audience. The stick is rotating on the bottom shaft of the pin. Bring the forefinger of your other hand down hard on the bottom end of the stick. The top

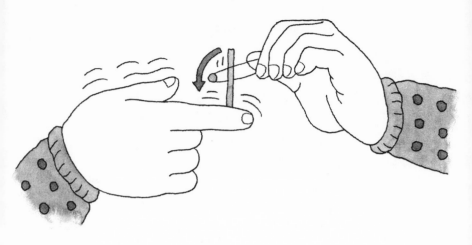

end will appear to move forward, toward you, through the top shaft of the pin. Reset the stick to the original position to repeat the illusion.

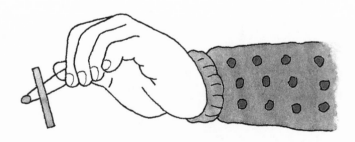

What's Really Happening

The stick moves forward against the top shaft and bounces off. It is the <u>bottom</u> end of the stick that winds up in front of the top shaft of the pin. It only appears that the stick moves through the steel shaft of the pin.

There are several things that contribute to the illusion. First, the human eye is incapable of seeing an object that is moving extremely fast. The motion of the stick is too quick to see.

Second, if the eye receives slightly different images of an object within a small fraction of a second, there is an illusion of motion. The viewer sees two images, one behind and one in front of the shaft of the pin. The brain puts the two images together to make it appear that there is a sequence to the motion.

The third thing that makes this trick work is that viewers have experience with the hand movement that sets the stick in motion. They believe that the downward motion of your finger should cause the top of the stick to move forward. They will not realize that the downward motion can produce a bounce, moving the bottom upward.

Since both ends of the stick are alike, the illusion is complete.

★
BENHAM'S TOP: A COLOR ILLUSION

You present a disk with a black-and-white design. Spin it and colors appear! Stop the spin and it's the same old black and white.

The Setup

☆ 7-inch white paper plates
☆ a pin
☆ scissors
☆ a ruler
☆ India ink and a pointed paintbrush
☆ a phonograph turntable or a pencil with a point or a knitting needle

The first problem is to find the exact center of a plate. Fold a paper plate exactly in half. Open it and fold it in half again in a different direction. The point where the two creases cross is the center of the plate.

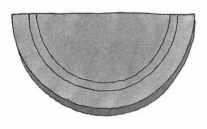
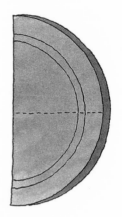

Stick a pin through at this point and lay this
plate on top of an uncreased plate. Use the pin
to mark the center.

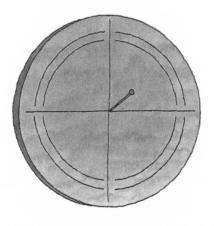

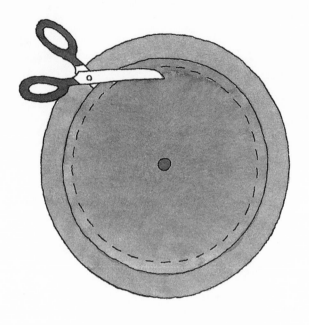

Trim the border from the uncreased plate. Using a ruler and India ink (you want the black to be very black), copy one of the black-and-white patterns shown in the illustration. You might want to try both patterns to see which works best for you. Enlarge the central hole so the disk fits on a phonograph turntable or will spin on a pencil point or knitting needle.

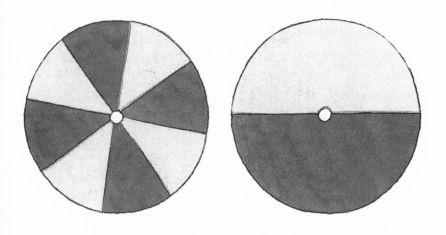

The Act

Show the black-and-white disk to your audience. Ask if anyone sees any colors on it. Then place it on a turntable under good lighting. It should rotate slowly. (You might find you get a better effect if you spin it by hand.) Instruct your audience to watch the disk and let you know when they start seeing colors and what colors they see.

Stop the turntable and point out that the disk is still only black and white.

Performance Tips: This is most effective as a close-up trick with a few friends.

You might want to investigate this illusion as a science project. Find out which speeds of rotation produce the illusion, how varying the amounts of black and white affects the colors people see, and if different people see different colors.

What's Really Happening

When light enters your eye, it passes through the eyeball to the back, where it strikes an area called the *retina*. The retina is packed with special light-sensitive cells.

Nerves connected to the light-sensitive cells fire in patterns that tell your brain what you are seeing. If the retina receives repeated flashes of white light for a short time, these nerves will fire in patterns your brain interprets as color. You see color where no color really exists.

When the black-and-white disk is spinning, it may be producing repeated flashes of light that can fool your brain. This phenomenon was discovered in the nineteenth century by a man named Benham who invented a black-and-white top, which was a very popular toy for a while.

No one really understands why Benham's top produces the illusion of color, although there are several unproved theories. The idea that the disk produces something like flashes of light causing the nerves that are sensitive to color to fire is the most popular explanation.

★

THE POSSESSED PENDULUM: A DEPTH ILLUSION

A pendulum known to be swinging from side to side can appear to be swinging in a circular path, sometimes clockwise and sometimes counterclockwise. The illusion is in the eye of the beholder.

The Setup and the Act

☆ a string about three feet long
☆ a heavy object to act as a pendulum bob
☆ dark glasses (I used an inexpensive package of ten sunglasses that were birthday-party favors. I cut the glasses in half so there were enough lenses for twenty people.)

Tie the string to the heavy object. Hang the pendulum in front of a blank wall. It should swing slowly from side to side.

Hand out dark lenses to members of your audience. Have them watch the pendulum swing with both eyes open. Ask someone to describe the path of the pendulum.

Then have everyone hold a dark lens in front of the right eye, keeping both eyes open. Have someone describe the motion of the pendulum. It will appear to be swinging in an oval path in a clockwise direction.

Then have everyone switch the lens to the left eye. The pendulum will appear to change its direction of rotation. It will seem to be swinging in an oval path in a counterclockwise direction.

Performance Tip: This is great entertainment for a party.

What's Really Happening

Brightness of an image affects the way light-sensitive cells in the retina respond. A very bright light causes nerves to fire a fraction of a second sooner than dimmer light.

In this trick, both eyes are looking at a moving object. One eye is covered with a dark lens so it will see an image that is less bright than the uncovered eye. The nerves in the retina of the uncovered eye send their message to the brain sooner than those in the other eye, producing an illusion of depth. Thus, you see the pendulum swinging in a circular path instead of simply back and forth. When you change the lens to the other eye, the pattern is reversed.

★
BIZARRE BOOMERANGS: A SIZE ILLUSION

You display two cardboard boomerangs and prove they are the same size by putting one on top of the other. Then you stretch one with your hands and, suddenly, it grows. Squeeze it and it shrinks.

The Setup

☆ 7-inch paper plates
☆ a pin
☆ a pencil
☆ scissors

Find the center of a paper plate as you did for Benham's Top (p. 132). Draw a pie-shaped wedge that extends to the center and includes about one third of the plate. Cut this piece out.

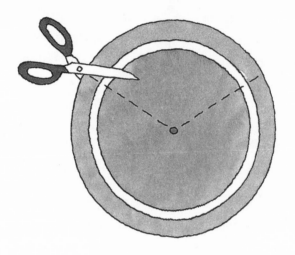

Use the outside arc of another plate as a pattern and draw an arc on the pie-shaped piece so that the straight edges are about 1½ inches long. Cut the pie-shaped piece along the smaller arc to form the boomerang. Use this boomerang as a pattern to make another one.

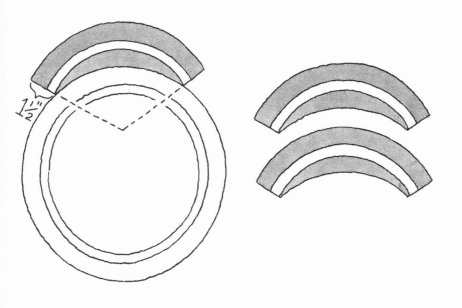

The Act

Show your audience that the two boomerangs are exactly the same size by putting one over the other. Put one boomerang down on the table. Pretend to stretch the other one. Show how the stretching has worked by comparing it to the boomerang you've left on the table. When you compare boomerangs, be sure to put the boomerang you pretended to stretch <u>under</u> the other boomerang.

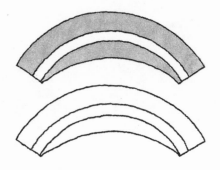

Performance Tips: You can elaborate on the trick by pretending to shrink the boomerang. When you put it back down, put it <u>above</u> the other boomerang, so it appears smaller than the one you haven't touched.

What's Really Happening

An object can appear to be larger or smaller without actually changing size depending on its surroundings. In this trick, the illusion that one boomerang is larger than the other is created by positioning the smaller arc of one boomerang above the larger arc of the other. The two arcs, which are next to each other, are different in size, so the two boomerangs look different in size. The lower boomerang appears to be larger. This illusion is so reliable that a demonstration that the two are exactly the same size doesn't change your perception that the upper boomerang is smaller than the lower one.

Another example of this illusion in nature is the apparent change in the size of a full moon as it rises. When the moon is near the horizon, it appears larger than it does later when it is overhead. One explanation is that it looks larger near the horizon because we see it along with familiar objects, like trees and buildings. If you look at the moon through a tube or a tiny window made of the thumbs and index fingers of both hands, which cuts out these other objects, the moon instantly shrinks. It appears to be the same smaller size that you see when it is high in the sky.

INDEX